LAURI

D0842933

BL 3.7
Pts OS

PET CARE LIBRARY

Caring for Your Turtle

by Colleen Sexton

BELLWETHER MEDIA · MINNEAPOLIS, MN

BLASTOFF!
READERS
4

Note to Librarians, Teachers, and Parents:

Blastoff! Readers are carefully developed by literacy experts and combine standards-based content with developmentally appropriate text.

Level 1 provides the most support through repetition of high-frequency words, light text, predictable sentence patterns, and strong visual support.

Level 2 offers early readers a bit more challenge through varied simple sentences, increased text load, and less repetition of high-frequency words.

Level 3 advances early-fluent readers toward fluency through increased text and concept load, less reliance on visuals, longer sentences, and more literary language.

Level 4 builds reading stamina by providing more text per page, increased use of punctuation, greater variation in sentence patterns, and increasingly challenging vocabulary.

Level 5 encourages children to move from "learning to read" to "reading to learn" by providing even more text, varied writing styles, and less familiar topics.

Whichever book is right for your reader, Blastoff! Readers are the perfect books to build confidence and encourage a love of reading that will last a lifetime!

This edition first published in 2011 by Bellwether Media, Inc.

No part of this publication may be reproduced in whole or in part without written permission of the publisher. For information regarding permission, write to Bellwether Media, Inc., Attention: Permissions Department, 5357 Penn Avenue South, Minneapolis, MN 55419.

Library of Congress Cataloging-in-Publication Data
Sexton, Colleen A., 1967-
Caring for your turtle / by Colleen Sexton.
p. cm. – (Blastoff! readers. Pet care library)
Summary: "Developed by literacy experts for students in grades two through five, this title provides readers with basic information for taking care of turtles"–Provided by publisher.
  Includes bibliographical references and index.
ISBN 978-1-60014-472-1 (hardcover : alk. paper)
1. Turtles as pets–Juvenile literature. I. Title.
SF459.T8S39 2010
639.3'92–dc22
                                            2010011482

Text copyright © 2011 by Bellwether Media, Inc. BLASTOFF! READERS and associated logos are trademarks and/or registered trademarks of Bellwether Media, Inc.

Printed in the United States of America, North Mankato, MN.
120110   1179

Contents

Choosing a Turtle

A turtle is a pet for a lifetime. Pet turtles can live for 50 years or more! Your turtle will depend on you to take care of it every day.

Turtles come in many sizes. Their bodies and shells can have different patterns and colors. Some turtles live only on land and some live mostly in water.

slider turtle

mud turtle

box turtle

fun fact

Some of the most popular
pet turtles are slider turtles,
mud turtles, map turtles,
and box turtles.

Not all turtles make good pets. Learn about the
different kinds of turtles and their needs. That will
help you choose the right turtle to bring home.

map turtle

Do not keep a wild turtle as a pet.
Instead, buy a turtle from a turtle **breeder**.
Their turtles make healthier pets.

A Home for Your Turtle

land turtle cage

You will need a lot of supplies
to properly care for a turtle.
Your turtle will need a large tank or
cage to live in. Make sure the tank or
cage is covered so your turtle can't escape.

A large cage gives land turtles room to explore, climb, and dig. Place a shallow bowl of water in the cage for drinking and bathing. Be sure to change the water every day.

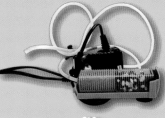
filter

Supply List

Here is a list of supplies you will need to take care of a turtle.

- **cage or tank**
- **food and water bowls**
- **bedding**
- **filter**
- **plants**
- **rocks**
- **heater**
- **heat lamp**
- **turtle food**

bedding

heat lamp

Cover the bottom of your land turtle's cage with newspaper, sand, soil, or other **bedding**. Scoop out your turtle's waste every day and change the bedding at least once a week.

bedding

Care Tip

Turtles grow throughout their lives. Your turtle might need a bigger home as it gets older.

Water turtles need a tank with a swimming area and a land area. The swimming area should have plenty of room for your turtle to move around.

The water in the swimming area should be as deep as your turtle is long. That will give your turtle space to flip over if it turns on its back. Being upside-down is not good for turtles.

Turtles need clean water in their swimming area to stay healthy. Put a **filter** in the tank to trap dirt and clean the water. Clean out the filter and change the water at least once each week.

filter

Care Tip

Turtles can carry a disease called salmonella. Always wash your hands after handling your turtle or cleaning its cage or tank.

The land area in the tank can be a large rock, a wooden shelf, or another flat place. It needs to be easy for your turtle to climb out of the water and onto the land area.

Both land turtles and water turtles like to hide. You can add plants, rocks, and other objects to your turtle's home to make hiding places. Check that the plants you use are safe for your turtle.

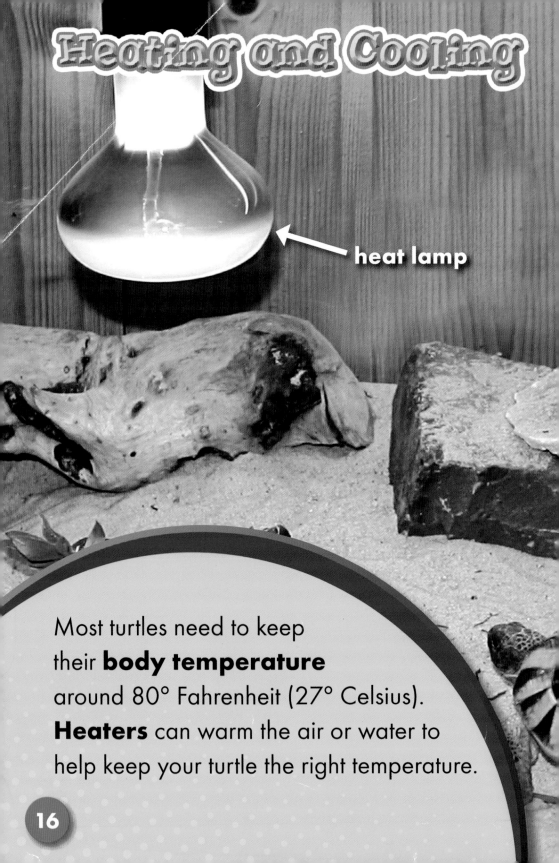

Heating and Cooling

heat lamp

Most turtles need to keep their **body temperature** around 80° Fahrenheit (27° Celsius). **Heaters** can warm the air or water to help keep your turtle the right temperature.

Turtle homes need warm spots and cool spots. Your turtle will want to **bask** in the light of a **heat lamp** to warm up. It will move into the water or to another spot to cool off.

fun fact

Turtles are cold-blooded. Their bodies are the same temperature as their surroundings.

Feed your turtle every two or three days. Most turtles eat fruits and vegetables. Many turtles like fish or meat. It is important to learn which foods are best for your type of turtle.

fun fact

Turtles don't have teeth.
They suck food into their
mouths or grab it with
their sharp jaws.

Watch your turtle closely for changes in its habits or appearance. Check regularly for cuts in your turtle's skin, cracks in its shell, or changes in its color. If it stops eating, it may be sick. Take it to a **veterinarian** for any of these problems.

Handling Your Turtle

Some turtles like people to pet their heads. However, most turtles don't like to be touched. They think that a predator is attacking them! Some turtles will hide inside their shells.

Pick your turtle up only when you need to move it. Watch your turtle instead of holding it. Seeing how your turtle eats, swims, and explores is fun!

Glossary

bask—to soak up heat from the sun or another source of light; basking helps turtles raise their body temperatures.

bedding—material laid down as a bed for an animal; changing the bedding helps keep a turtle's home clean.

body temperature—the amount of heat in a turtle's body; a turtle has a body temperature that is the same as its surroundings.

breeder—a person who raises turtles and sells them to other people

filter—a device that water passes through; a filter removes chemicals and waste from water.

heat lamp—a lamp designed to give off a lot of heat; turtles move under heat lamps to warm up.

heaters—machines that produce warmth to heat air or water

veterinarian—a doctor who takes care of animals

To Learn More

AT THE LIBRARY
Algarra, Alejandro. *Let's Take Care of Our New Turtle*. Hauppauge, N.Y.: Barron's Educational, 2008.

Hamilton, Lynn. *Caring for Your Turtle*. New York, N.Y.: Weigl Publishers, 2004.

Stevens, Kathryn. *Turtles*. Mankato, Minn.: Child's World, 2009.

ON THE WEB
Learning more about pet care is as easy as 1, 2, 3.

1. Go to www.factsurfer.com.

2. Enter "pet care" into the search box.

3. Click the "Surf" button and you will see a list of related Web sites.

With factsurfer.com, finding more information is just a click away.

Index

The images in this book are reproduced through the courtesy of: Gerald A. DeBoer, front cover; Robert Dant, front cover (small); Image Source/Getty Images, pp. 4-5, 20-21; Juan Martinez, pp. 6 (top, middle), 9 (top), 12 (small); Robert Ranson, p. 6 (bottom); C Steimer/Age Fotostock, pp. 6-7, 8-9, 10, 11, 12-13, 14, 15; Iwona Grodzka, p. 9 (middle); Juniors Bildarchiv/Photolibray, pp. 9 (bottom), 16-17; Juniors Bildarchiv/Alamy, pp. 18-19; Germán Ariel Berra, p. 19 (small).